DINOSAURS

Open up and say **"ROAAAAR!"** Get ready for a trip far, far back in time, to an age when unimaginably giant creatures called dinosaurs ruled the Earth. Living during different time periods, on different parts of the planet, these animals are known to us today only by the fossils (preserved body parts) that they left behind. Scientists study these fossils to learn about dinosaurs' looks and lifestyles. In these pages, we'll take a look at some of the facts scientists have uncovered.

GIGANTORAPTOR

To say the dinosaur's name, try sounding it out like this: "jih-GAN-toe-RAP-tore."

Gigantoraptor belongs to the oviraptor group. "Oviraptor" means "egg thief" because scientists once thought that these dinosaurs stole eggs from other dinosaurs' nests. Today they know this is not true. Oviraptors laid eggs in their own nests and tended them, just like modern birds do. In fact, these dinosaurs are closely related to birds. They even had some feathers!

Gigantoraptor didn't have as many feathers as other members of the group. It is likely that its skin was mostly bare, with just a few long feathers on the forearms, head, and tail. It probably used these feathers for display and to keep its eggs warm.

The nesting process must have been an amazing sight, because Gigantoraptor was enormous! It was up to 28 feet (8.6m) long and 11.5 feet (3.5m) tall, and its eggs were up to 21 inches (53cm) long. That's one big "bird" for sure.

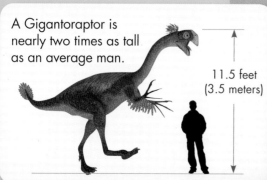

A Gigantoraptor is nearly two times as tall as an average man.

11.5 feet
(3.5 meters)

DID YOU KNOW?
A Gigantoraptor egg is 21 inches (53 cm) tall. It is over 3 times taller than an ostrich egg and 10 times taller than a chicken egg.

Gigantoraptor Facts

Timespan: 84–71 million years ago
Length: 28 feet (8.6 meters)
Height: 11.5 feet (3.5 meters)
Food Source: Herbivore (An herbivore only eats plants.)
Extra Info: Discovered in Inner Mongolia, China, in 2005. Had birdlike beak and claws. Could run at 20 mph (32 kph).

SUCHOMIMUS

(SOO-koe-MIME-us)

This dinosaur's name comes from Greek words meaning "crocodile mimic." Scientists chose this name because they thought Suchomimus had a crocodile-like skull. The skull, along with about two-thirds of a skeleton, was discovered in Niger, Africa, in 1997. This part of Africa is a desert today. But 113 million years ago, when Suchomimus roamed the Earth, this area was a swamp—the perfect habitat for this water-loving dinosaur.

How do we know this? Suchomimus's powerful tail and flattened body position are clues to its lifestyle. Like the crocodiles for which it is named, Suchomimus spent most of its time in the water. It often waded through creeks and ponds, using its powerful jaws to snap up fish. It may have also sat on riverbanks and used its sharp, curved claws to hook prey.

With its long, crocodile-like snout and huge thumb claws, Suchomimus looked like a mixture of a T. rex, a Spinosaurus, and a crocodile.

DID YOU KNOW? Suchomimus had 122 sharply pointed teeth that it used mainly to eat large amounts of fish.

Suchomimus Facts

Timespan: 125–112 million years ago
Length: 31 feet (9.5 meters)
Weight: 2.5 tons (2.3 tonnes)
Food Source: Carnivore (A carnivore eats meat.)
Extra Info: Only one Suchomimus specimen has ever been found.

STEGOSAURUS

(STEG-uh-SORE-us)

Stegosaurus is a very easy dinosaur to recognize. The large, bony plates on this creature's back are a giveaway! In fact, Stegosaurus gets its name, which means "covered lizard," from these plates.

Along with its magnificent back plates, Stegosaurus also had dangerous spikes on its tail. Scientists believe that this dinosaur used its plates and spikes to defend itself. If attacked, the usually gentle Stegosaurus swung its mighty tail like a club to wallop its enemies into submission. Spike-shaped wounds in predator fossils support this theory.

Stegosaurus fossils were first found in 1877, making this dinosaur one of the older species to be named. It lived in the area that is now the western United States and possibly also in Europe during the late Jurassic period.

DID YOU KNOW?
The collection of four to ten spikes on a Stegosaurus's tail is called a thagomizer.

Each Stegosaurus had 17 plates on its back. The largest plates measured about 2x2 feet (61x61cm). Scientists believe the plates helped to balance Stegosaurus's body temperature.

Stegosaurus Facts

Timespan: 156–151 million years ago

Length: 30 feet (9 meters)

Height: 13 feet (4 meters)

Food Source: Herbivore

Extra Info: Stegosaurus had a tipped-forward posture because its front legs were shorter than its back legs. It had a very small head.

DICRAEOSAURUS

(dy-KRAY-uh-SORE-us)

Dicraeosaurus fossils have been found in Tanzania, Africa and in Argentina, South America. When Dicraeosaurus roamed the Earth more than 150 million years ago, these countries were part of the same continent!

Dicraeosaurus's most unique feature is a double row of spikes down the back. These spikes might have been used for defense—predators would not want to bite down onto this living pincushion! The spikes also might have attached to a fin or sail. No one knows for sure.

What we do know is that Dicraeosaurus was a grazer. This dinosaur lived alongside two other grazing species. One species was much taller than Dicraeosaurus, and one was much shorter. Each type of dinosaur grazed only at its own height, leaving plenty of food for the others. That's lucky for Dicraeosaurus, which needed lots of chow to keep its 40-foot body healthy!

DID YOU KNOW?
Since Dicraeosaurus had no armor or sharp claws to protect itself, it may have used its long tail as a whip.

Dicraeosaurus Facts

Timespan: 156–151 million years ago
Length: 40 feet (12 meters)
Weight: 5 tons (5.5 tonnes)
Food Source: Herbivore
Extra Info: The first Dicraeosaurus fossil was described by Werner Janensch in 1914. Its name means "double forked lizard."

PACHYCEPHALOSAURUS

(pak-ee-SEF-uh-low-SORE-us)

Pachycephalosaurus remains have been found in modern-day Wyoming, Montana, and South Dakota. This omnivore walked on its two hind legs and had a very thick skull.

Length: 15 feet (4.5 meters)
Weight: 990 pounds (450 kg)

STEGOCERAS

(STEG-uh-SARE-us)

Stegoceras was a plant eater, but scientists think it was a fierce fighter nonetheless. They believe Stegoceras used its extra-thick head to whack rivals during battles over territory, food, and mates.

Height: 6.6 feet (2 meters)
Weight: 88 pounds (40 kg)

DIMETRODON

(dy-MEET-ruh-don)

Dimetrodon is best known for the large sail it carried on its back. It was not a true dinosaur. It was more closely related to mammals than reptiles, and it died out 40 million years before the first dinosaurs appeared.

Length: 15 feet (4.6 meters)
Weight: 550 pounds (250 kg)

CERATOSAURUS

(sur-AT-uh-SORE-us)

Ceratosaurus means "horned lizard," and it's easy to see why. This dinosaur had a horn on its nose! Ceratosaurus was a powerful predator with mighty rear legs and tiny forearms.

Length: 20 feet (6.2 meters)

Weight: 1,500 pounds (700 kg)

GIGANTSPINOSAURUS

(jy-gant-SPINE-uh-SORE-us)

Gigantspinosaurus belonged to the Stegosaur family. This small herbivore had a unique built-in defense: two giant spikes sticking out of its shoulder blades!

Length: 14 feet (4.2 meters)

Weight: 1,500 pounds (700 kg)

PHORUSRHACOS

(FOR-us-RAK-us)

Phorusrhacos was a giant predatory bird. This brute terrorized the woodlands and grasslands of Patagonia, using its sharp, hooked beak to rip prey to shreds.

Height: 8.2 feet (2.5 meters)

Weight: 290 pounds (130 kg)

NEDOCERATOPS

(NED-uh-SARE-uh-tops)

With a bony, frilled neck plate and sharp horns sticking up from its brow, Nedoceratops was an impressive creature. So why does this dinosaur's name mean "insufficient horn face"? Because poor Nedoceratops only had two horns, unlike its better-known cousin, Triceratops, which boasted three!

Nedoceratops lived in the area that is now Wyoming. It is known from only one fossil skull, which was discovered in 1905. Paleontologists originally thought the skull was missing its nose horn due to injury or disease. Closer examination proved that this was not the case. The skull was perfect—just different.

The missing horn probably didn't bother Nedoceratops much. This mighty herbivore had no trouble protecting itself while it grazed on ferns and conifers. The beast used its sharp beak to strip tasty leaves or needles from tough branches.

DiD YOU KNOW?
Nedoceratops has had a name change. Until 2007, this dinosaur was known as Diceratops.

HEY!
MY NAME IS

Ned

Nedoceratops Facts

Timespan: 67–66 million years ago
Length: 25 feet (7.6 meters)
Height: 7 feet (2.2 meters)
Food Source: Herbivore
Extra Info: Some scientists think the single existing Nedoceratops skull is actually the skull of a young Triceratops whose nose horn has not yet grown in.

SPINOSAURUS

(SPiNE-uh-SORE-us)

Spinosaurus might be the largest, most fearsome predator ever to have walked our planet. This humongous meat eater was up to 59 feet long and may have weighed as much as 21 tons (23 tonnes). Comfortable both on land and in the water, Spinosaurus gobbled down whatever prey it could find, wherever it could find it. Fish and smaller dinosaurs made up most of this giant's diet.

Besides its vast size, Spinosaurus is also recognized by the magnificent sail on its back. The sail was anchored by bony spikes that stuck up from the spine. A tough layer of skin connected the spikes, like the webbing between a duck's toes. Spinosaurus might have used this sail to regulate its body temperature and to intimidate enemies.

DiD YOU KNOW?
The Spinosaurus was larger than the Tyrannosaurus Rex. It also may have been the largest carnivorous dinosaur.

The sail on a Spinosaurus is a little shorter than the height as an average man.

5 feet
(1.5 m)

Psittacosaurus

Spinosaurus Facts

Timespan: 99–94 million years ago
Length: 59 feet (18 meters)
Weight: 21 tons (23 tonnes)
Food Source: Carnivore
Extra Info: Name means "spine lizard."
Lived in the area that is now North
Africa. First discovered in Egypt in 1912.

ELASMOSAURUS

(ell-AZ-muh-SORE-us)

Elasmosaurus was a type of marine reptile called a plesiosaur. Elasmosaurus had a long, snakelike neck with 71 vertebrae. This plesiosaur was a slow swimmer that followed schools of fish in the open sea. It had flipperlike paddles instead of arms and legs and could not have come onto the land.

MOSASAURUS

(MOZE-uh-SORE-us)

Mosasaurus was the opposite of Elasmosaurus in some ways. It had a short, strong neck and was a fast swimmer. It stuck mostly to shallow water, hunting for fish, turtles, and possibly smaller Mosasauruses. Mosasaurus belonged to the mosasaur group, which resembled modern crocodiles.

DID YOU KNOW?
Predators that eat mostly fish are called piscivores.

Elasmosaurus

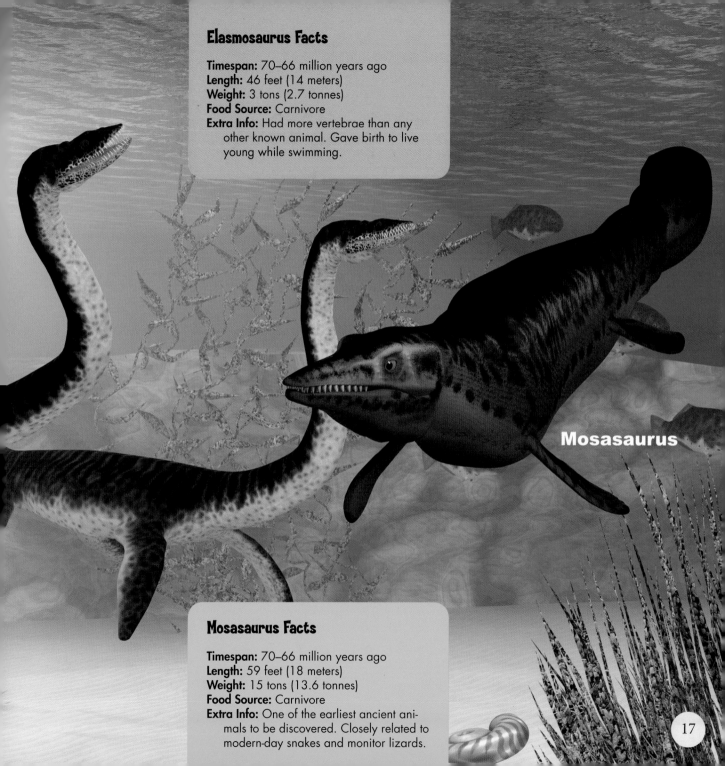

Elasmosaurus Facts

Timespan: 70–66 million years ago
Length: 46 feet (14 meters)
Weight: 3 tons (2.7 tonnes)
Food Source: Carnivore
Extra Info: Had more vertebrae than any
other known animal. Gave birth to live
young while swimming.

Mosasaurus

Mosasaurus Facts

Timespan: 70–66 million years ago
Length: 59 feet (18 meters)
Weight: 15 tons (13.6 tonnes)
Food Source: Carnivore
Extra Info: One of the earliest ancient ani-
mals to be discovered. Closely related to
modern-day snakes and monitor lizards.

PSITTACOSAURUS
(SiT-uh-kuh-SORE-us)

This dinosaur is very well known to scientists. Fossils of over 400 individuals have been collected so far! These small plant eaters had powerful, birdlike jaws and tall bristles on their tails.

Length: 6.6 feet (2 meters)

Weight: 50 pounds (22 kg)

PTERANODON
(tur-ANN-uh-don)

Pteranodon was a flying reptile, not a bird. This predator had very long wings compared to its body, similar in proportion to the modern albatross. It mostly soared, with occasional bursts of flapping.

Length: 24 feet (7.3 meters)

Weight: 110 pounds (50 kg)

PARASAUROLOPHUS
(PARE-uh-SORE-uh-LOW-fus)

Parasaurolophus is easily recognized by the long, curved crest that arches off the back of its head. This dinosaur could walk both on its two hind legs or on all four legs. Parasaurolophus lived in large herds on grassy plains. It used its flat teeth to grind tough plant matter.

Length: 33 feet (10 meters)

Weight: 2.5 tons (2.3 tonnes)

CAMARASAURUS

(CAM-uh-ruh-SORE-us)

Like all sauropods, Camarasaurus had a long neck, a long tail, a small head, and elephantlike legs. This gentle giant was a common herbivore in the area that is now North America. With teeth shaped like chisels, it could eat very tough plant materials.

Length: 75 feet (23 meters)
Weight: 32 tons (29 tonnes)

UTAHRAPTOR

(YOU-tah-rap-tore)

Utahraptor was not big by dinosaur standards, but it was ferocious. This feathered predator used the large, curved claws on its second toes to attack its prey.

Length: 23 feet (7 meters)
Weight: 990 pounds (450 kg)

PACHYRHINOSAURUS

(PACK-ee-RiNE-uh-SORE-us)

This small ceratopsid had a bony frill circling its neck, like a collar. The frill was topped with sharp, curved horns. Pachyrhinosaurus ("thick-nosed reptile") used its horns to defend itself from larger predators.

Length: 26 feet (8 meters)
Weight: 3 tons (2.7 tonnes)

MAMENCHISAURUS

(ma-MEN-chih-SORE-us)

Mamenchisaurus is known for its amazingly long neck, which accounted for about half of the dinosaur's length. And what a length! One of the largest sauropods, Mamenchisaurus measured up to 115 feet (35 meters) from nose to tail tip.

Like other sauropods, Mamenchisaurus was an herbivore. This huge plant eater roamed an area that is now part of China, looking for tasty vegetation to eat. Scientists think Mamenchisaurus's vast neck came in handy for this task.

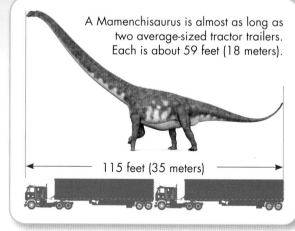

A Mamenchisaurus is almost as long as two average-sized tractor trailers. Each is about 59 feet (18 meters).

115 feet (35 meters)

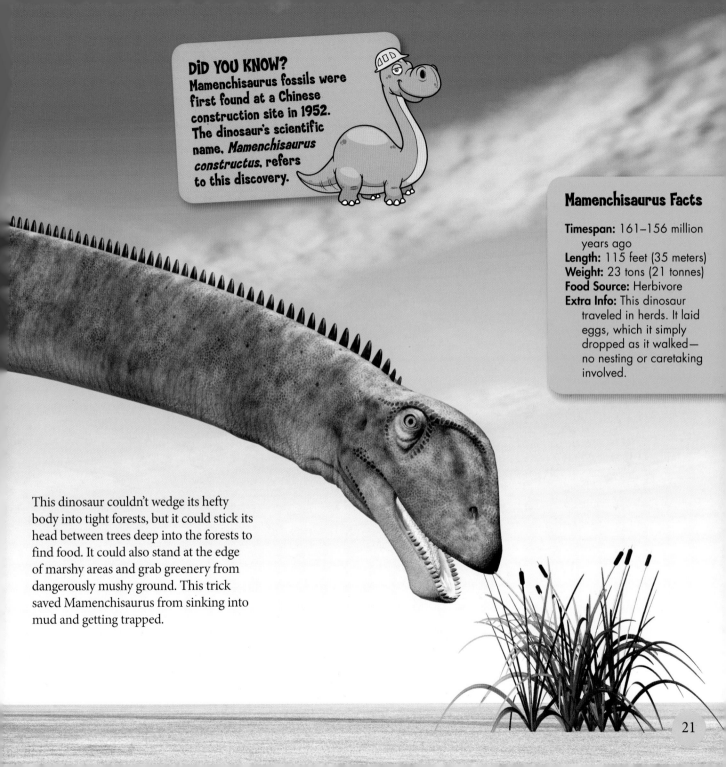

Mamenchisaurus Facts

Timespan: 161–156 million years ago
Length: 115 feet (35 meters)
Weight: 23 tons (21 tonnes)
Food Source: Herbivore
Extra Info: This dinosaur traveled in herds. It laid eggs, which it simply dropped as it walked— no nesting or caretaking involved.

This dinosaur couldn't wedge its hefty body into tight forests, but it could stick its head between trees deep into the forests to find food. It could also stand at the edge of marshy areas and grab greenery from dangerously mushy ground. This trick saved Mamenchisaurus from sinking into mud and getting trapped.

TYRANNOSAURUS

(tie-RAN-uh-SORE-us)

The word "Tyrannosaurus" refers to a whole family of dinosaurs. The best-known member of the family is Tyrannosaurus Rex, which means "tyrant lizard king." This vicious predator was by far the largest and meanest hunter in the area that is now western North America. It ate any smaller creature it could catch. It was happy to grab the occasional "fast food" meal, too, stealing and eating other dinosaurs' kills whenever it could.

Tyrannosaurus had strong but tiny forearms, so its main hunting tools were its speed and teeth. This dinosaur used its powerful hind legs to overtake prey. When it caught up, it used its massive jaws and teeth to deliver a killing bite. Scientists believe that Tyrannosaurus might have had the strongest bite of any animal that has ever lived on Earth.

Tooth root

Tyrannosaurus had about 60 massive, banana-shaped teeth. The largest known Tyrannosaur tooth is about 12 inches (30 cm) long, including the root.

Tyrannosaurus Facts

Timespan: 67–66 million years ago
Length: 44 feet (13.3 meters)
Weight: 7.7 tons (7 tonnes)
Food Source: Carnivore
Extra Info: Most scientists think Tyrannosaurus had at least some feathers. This big beast is related to modern birds!

DID YOU KNOW?

"Sue," a fossilized Tyrannosaurus on display at the Field Museum in Chicago, is one of the most complete dinosaur skeletons ever found. The specimen includes 80 percent of its original bones.

VELOCIRAPTOR

(vel-AH-sih-RAP-tore)

The real Velociraptor was smaller and less fierce than the one seen in some modern movies. This feathered hunter did, however, have the curved toe claws featured in films. Velociraptor used these claws to snag and tear prey such as reptiles, amphibians, and smaller, slower dinosaurs. It lived and hunted in the area that is now Mongolia, China.

Velociraptor Facts

Timespan: 84–71 million years ago
Length: 6 feet (1.8 meters)
Weight: 40 pounds (18 kg)
Food Source: Carnivore
Extra Info: Had a long, low skull with an upturned snout. Often called simply a "raptor."

Images used from shutterstock: Cover: DM7 - Page 1: Ralf Juergen Kraft - Pages 2-3: Kostyantyn Ivanyshen, Valentyna\Chukhlyebova - Pages 4-5: Kostyantyn Ivanyshen, DM7, Linda Bucklin, Andrew Burgess - Pages 6-7: Linda Bucklin, leonello calvetti, Michael Rosskothen - Pages 8-9: Kostyantyn Ivanyshen - Pages 10-11: leonello calvetti, Michael Rosskothen, leonello calvetti, DM7, Michael Rosskothen, Catmando - Pages 12-13: DM7 - Pages 14-15: Linda Bucklin, Linda Bucklin - Pages 16-17: Catmando, Ralf Juergen Kraft - Pages 18-19: Linda Bucklin, Ralf Juergen Kraft, Jean-Michel Girard, Linda Bucklin, Ralf Juergen Kraft, Linda Bucklin - Pages 20-21: Michael Rosskothen, Michael Rosskothen, - Pages 22-23: Kostyantyn Ivanyshen, DM7, Marco Cavina, Teguh Mujiono - Page 24 : Michael Rosskothen - Back cover: Linda Bucklin, Jean-Michel Girard